Road To Success

A Few Things You Need to Know

Mohammed R Ahmed

Copyright © 2024 Mohammed R Ahmed
All rights reserved

The characters and events portrayed in this book are fictitious. Any similarity to real persons, living or dead, is coincidental and not intended by the author.

No part of this book may be reproduced, or stored in a retrieval system, or transmitted in any form or by any means, electronic, mechanical, photocopying, recording, or otherwise, without express written permission of the publisher.

ISBN-13: 979-8-9908963-5-2

Cover design by: Author
Library of Congress Control Number: 2024912655
Printed in the United States of America

DEDICATION

This book is dedicated to the loving memory of our grandson Alex, who was craving his way to the road to success.

EPIGRAPH

Energy kickstarts the journey of life.
Using energy without a goal is a waste of energy.
Energy fuels both positive and negative outcomes.
Knowing a few things about energy will help you succeed.
Managing energy increases the chance of success.

Mohammed R Ahmed

CONTENTS

Title Page	i
Copyright	ii
Dedication	iii
Epigraph	iv
Preface	vii
Introduction	ix
Energy	1
Growth	8
Emotions	13
Trust	20
Responsibility	27
Learning	33
Dreams	37
Intelligence	42
Success	55
About the Author	59

PREFACE

I have written several short articles and shared my views in the classroom and public forums on various topics that help individuals carve the path to success. These writings were based on the topic of interest at a particular time, event, or need to share information and knowledge with the learners. A recent review of my collection of articles made me realize several articles, when presented together, provide useful information for readers to manage human energy and use it for positive outcomes. I selected these interconnected areas and shared a few things from articles to help individuals carve the path to success. As a result, a short book was named Road to Success, with a table of contents reflecting the selected areas composed for the digital age readers.

Everything we do in life requires energy, but we do not focus on managing it because it is invisible. No one can track its usage or pay for it because it is naturally generated by the human body. The book focuses on critical areas that consume high energy and areas that result in negative outcomes if energy is not managed. A better understanding of these areas and proper energy management will lead to the road to success.

INTRODUCTION

Energy is the power behind actions. Everyone can learn how to manage human energy to minimize negative and maximize positive outcomes.

We had a family get-together, and one of our great-granddaughters loved to view family pictures on my wife's phone. She was viewing pictures on the phone and saw several apps and web browser pages open, and said Nana, if you leave these apps and pages open, you will lose the battery quickly. She showed her how to close the apps and the open pages to save energy. I was impressed with the 10-year-old, who was tech-savvy and concerned about saving energy. She was aware of energy consumption issues because she had a cell phone and understood without power, a cell phone is a piece of equipment, and you cannot do anything. When we are traveling, my wife is always concerned about using maps for directions or watching movies on the phone during the flight because it drains the cell phone's battery. When driving, we always monitor the car's fuel (energy) indicator and refill it before it runs out. We also take a short route to work to save gas and reduce traveling expenses.

This raised my concern about why people are not concerned about human energy consumption, although the human body runs on energy. A reasonable explanation is that human energy is invisible and naturally generated without monetary cost. No fuel indicator is attached to the body to show the energy level, how much was used, and when to refill. We should be concerned about human energy because it fuels our human journey. Learning how to manage energy helps you to get on the road to success.

The human body is a fascinating, naturally made intelligent

machine, and we must understand how much energy is used to accomplish different tasks. There are twenty-four hours in a day and most of the time, the average individual works eight hours a day and sleeps eight hours, while the other eight hours are used for traveling to and from work, shopping, spending time with family, and others. The three main tasks humans are involved in that consume energy are mental, physical, and emotional. We need energy to work and make money and energy while sleeping to keep the body functioning and conducting other activities. Humans have limited energy, but our body has a built-in charging system for charging as we use the energy. We learn consciously or unconsciously how much energy to use for specific tasks to arrive at an outcome. Our goal should be to identify where energy could be used to achieve positive outcomes and reduce the use of energy where a large amount is used to arrive at negative outcomes.

We can learn from the energy consumption process of the cell phone and apply it to the energy process of humans to accomplish tasks. Leaving apps and web pages open on the cell phone consumes energy, and nothing is accomplished, which is a waste of energy and a negative outcome. On the other hand, if the cellphone is used for video conferences with colleagues, watching a movie, or purchasing things needed online, the energy will be used for a positive outcome. This book first discusses energy, the role of internal and external triggers, three common tasks individuals use energy, and energy consumption areas that mostly result in negative outcomes. The goal is to understand high energy areas consumption, such as personal growth, managing emotions, individual responsibility, and climbing the hierarchy of learning and dreaming, which requires management of the use of energy to minimize the negative outcome and maximize the positive outcome. The successful management of energy and emotions will create synergy in intelligence. Thus, leading to the road to success.

ENERGY

Energy gives us the power to laugh, cry, enjoy, compete, and succeed. We should learn how to use it to get on the road to success.

We experience the power of energy that fuels human life when a child starts crying or observing physical movements at birth. Mothers experience the energy of the child when the child turns in the womb during pregnancy. Natural energy powers the individual life journey, and we decide how to use it. Most of the time, we take our energy for granted because it is produced naturally. At the same time, there is no accountability on how much energy we use, how we use it, and what we have accomplished using it. We can learn about human energy consumption by examining how machines consume energy because humans are naturally built intelligent machines. Let's look at man-made machines such as automobiles that need gas (energy) to move from one place to another. Let's assume you wish to travel 350 miles, and your car has an 18-gallon gas tank and an average mileage of 20 miles per gallon on the highway, which has a speed limit of 70 miles per hour. You can reach your destination in five hours. You can also manage the energy consumption by controlling your route and speed. However, if you drive faster than 70 miles per hour or take a longer route, you may consume more gas (energy) and risk running out of gas on the highway and not reaching the destination. The two internal factors that determine a car's energy consumption are speed and distance. The external factors that may affect energy consumption are traffic density, wind or rain, and the condition of the road.

Let's learn from machines and apply the concept to human energy management. The energy individuals possess is called internal energy, and the energy surrounding them is called external energy. The three internal factors determining human energy consumption are physical, mental, and emotional tasks. Like a car's gas tank, our body has an energy retention system and refuels itself. But we don't have to go to a gas station to fill up or plug into an outlet to charge; our body is a self-charging machine. How we perform physical and mental tasks determines the energy needed to accomplish the task. The emotional intensity determines the amount of energy we consume and the speed at which it is consumed. Our goal should always be to use a minimal amount of energy and perform a maximum number of tasks. We can manage our mental, physical, and emotional tasks or refuel by regulating energy use.

We can learn from our personal experience how we use our energy and develop a system to efficiently utilize the energy to accomplish goals and succeed in life. Let me share an experience that may help you understand how we can manage our energy to accomplish a task. I was attending an annual professional management conference in a metropolitan city. The meeting was scheduled to start at 8:00 a.m., so I left my hotel a few minutes before 8:00 a.m. to walk the few blocks to the convention center. When I left the hotel, I encountered a panhandler who asked me for money. I politely apologized for not having any cash with me. The guy got upset, and as soon as I passed him, he shouted a few bad words. I had three choices: 1) keep walking and get to the meeting as quickly as possible, 2) shout back at him, or 3) go back inside the hotel and ask the concierge to move the man away from the front of the hotel. All three choices required my energy. He may have shouted back at me or engaged in a physical altercation if I had shouted back at him. I would have wasted my energy on mental and physical tasks and fueling emotions (anger). If I had gone back inside to complain to the concierge and ask him to do something about the panhandlers, I would have again wasted my energy on physical, mental, and emotional fueling. I kept walking because it was the best alternative for managing my energy. That morning, my goal was to share my research at the meeting and gain knowledge by interacting with other researchers. I used the saved energy to walk a few blocks (a physical task), recall my plan for sharing my research (a mental task), and give an energetic and pleasant presentation. The presentation went well, and the response from the audience refueled my energy. Sharing and gaining knowledge at the meeting was a great intellectual experience.

You can manage your energy if you understand that a trigger initiates energy consumption. A trigger leads to mental, physical, or emotional tasks. Sometimes, in tasks that involve positive emotions, the energy is refueled. Negative emotions mostly result in energy loss, impacting future mental, physical, and emotional tasks. We start using energy as soon as internal and external triggers occur. Triggers lead to positive or negative outcomes, and we use our energy knowingly or unknowingly for physical, mental, and emotional tasks and refueling. Each task we perform in our daily lives is different, and it may involve a mental, physical, emotional, or a combination to arrive at a desired outcome. Although we expect to arrive at the desired outcome, there is a chance of undesired outcomes occurring. As a rational individual, you need to understand that energy loss has occurred, recharge, and use your energy for the next desired outcome. The following exhibit shows triggers that initiate individual energy consumption and the types of tasks needed to achieve the desired outcomes.

Exhibit-1: Energy and Tasks

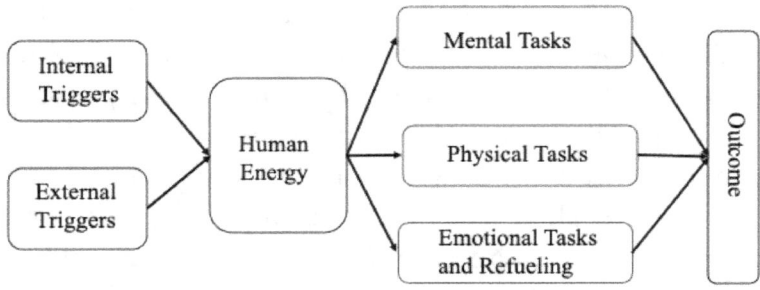

©2016 Mohammed R. Ahmed

Let's look at the automobile example again. Once you crank the ignition, the car starts consuming energy. It also consumes energy from the battery when parked to keep the clock, remote control, and other parts running. We also begin consuming energy while resting to keep our bodies functioning and when something triggers us.

In the above example of walking to the meeting, my internal trigger was the reminder that the meeting started at 8:00 a.m. This trigger led me to the physical task of walking toward the convention center and the mental task of planning the presentation while walking. I was also emotionally charged with excitement. The external trigger was the interaction with the panhandler. As an individual, you must evaluate internal and external triggers and learn to respond to triggers using energy to bring positive outcomes.

If I had responded to the initial interaction with the panhandler by entering a longer interaction, I would have wasted my energy and impacted my presentation. Managing my response to the external trigger helped me to preserve energy and achieve a positive outcome.

Four Steps for Managing Your Energy:

1. Understanding how to use internal energy for individual physical and mental tasks and emotional outcomes.
2. Learning how to use internal energy to respond to the energies exerted by external sources such as family, friends, coworkers, and the surrounding environment.
3. Conduct a self-audit to see how much energy you use to improve your life and how much you are wasting thinking about things, people, or actions that result in energy consumption without any benefits.
4. Use the audit results to change how you use your energy and focus on achieving your goals.

Let's assume you have a full gas tank in your car, and you can use the energy (gas) to go to the fitness center, work, movie theater, visit friends or family, or a restaurant. You can also use the energy (gas) to drive around the city without any goals and get stressed. Do not waste your energy just driving around without a goal because you will burn up gas and accomplish nothing. Your energy is more valuable than the gas in the car. Use it to improve your personal and professional life.

Every human being has energy, but the level of energy may differ from individual to individual based on one's biological formation. Humans regularly experience emotions such as happiness, love, surprise, sadness, fear, and anger, and we use energy to go through these emotions. We also use energy for physical and mental tasks. Our bodies are unique machines that produce the energy used for these tasks. For example, if you were to work in the yard for four hours mowing the lawn, you would feel tired and have no energy when you were finished. After resting for a few hours, you may feel better and be able to have fun with friends and family. This is an excellent example of how the body generates and uses energy to allow us to function as human beings. As a human being, you must learn how to manage your energy and direct it toward the appropriate physical and emotional tasks.

The road to success requires planning, and the purpose of this book is to share a few things necessary for preparing yourself to succeed in life. Several areas are essential for succeeding, but few identified areas are critical because they relate to the use or refueling of energy. Again, you can build an automobile with state-of-the-art technology, but if you cannot find the energy, whether gas or electricity, to run the car, you will not be on the road. It is the same for human beings. You will be off the road if you cannot learn how to use individual energy. Several things occur in our lives, and they require energy. This does not mean we need to monitor each activity to determine the optimal energy use. We need to focus on areas where a large amount of human energy is consumed to determine whether the use of energy is turning into positive outcomes. Once you learn how to manage energy use, you will be on the road to success. The following exhibit shows the critical areas that help individuals understand what is involved in joining the road to success.

Exhibit-2: Few Things Critical for Managing Energy

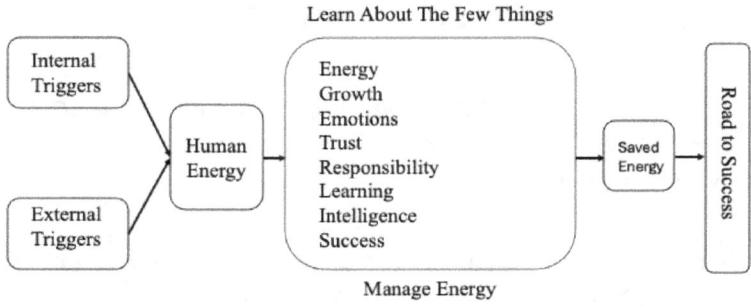

©2020 Mohammed R. Ahmed

We know internal and external triggers initiate energy consumption, and tasks may involve physical, mental, and emotional energy. Some areas may involve high and some low energy consumption. The individual goal should be to focus on high-energy consumption areas to optimize energy use and increase the chance of positive outcomes at a higher rate. It may sound like we are optimizing a machine, and it is, in fact, the human body, which is a machine made by nature. The book introduces you to the areas of high energy consumption so that you understand how energy is consumed, learn to manage energy, and use the saved energy to achieve your individual goals and succeed in life. This is why a few things, such as managing energy, personal growth, managing emotions, building trust, understanding responsibility, consequences for actions, learning for growth, dreams, and total intelligence, are included in this book. Understanding these few things will help you save energy and use it in the areas most essential to your life. In the next chapter, let's examine the variables involved in personal growth and learn why we need to manage energy to achieve growth.

GROWTH

Personal growth changes your life and makes you feel like you are out of the cage and free like a bird to continue exploring.

The word "growth" can have many meanings depending on the context. Our transformation from childhood to adulthood is an example of physical growth. Human beings undergo tangible or visible physical and intangible growth, such as mental, emotional, intellectual, and spiritual growth. Intangible growth gives human beings power, but it requires individual energy management.

Personal growth evolves and involves learning. It is a continuous process in which motivation and a growth mindset are crucial. Personal growth is attained through mental, emotional, intellectual, and spiritual growth. It is distinct from any other type of growth. For example, when we plant a seed, a tree will grow, thus providing shade, making the landscape beautiful, and helping boost our ecosystem. This is an example of tangible or visible growth, in which the physical changes throughout a life cycle can be seen. The life cycles of humans and other organisms have four phases: introduction, growth, maturity, and decline. In the case of plants, after you sow a seed, roots will grow, and then a tiny plant will appear above the ground. This is the introduction stage. The growth stage is the time it takes for a plant to grow into a full tree. The tree matures when it becomes fully grown or bears flowers or fruits. Once the tree starts decaying, it reaches what is referred to as the declining stage, which leads to the end of its life.

Human beings also go through the four stages of life: birth, growth, maturity, and decline. However, there is a stark difference between humans and other organisms on Earth. Human beings have a mind, body, and soul. By contrast, a tree only has a "body" and goes through a natural growth process. This is why the focus is only on physical growth. The following exhibit shows the variable of personal growth and motivation, and maturity plays a role in personal growth.

Exhibit-3: Personal Growth

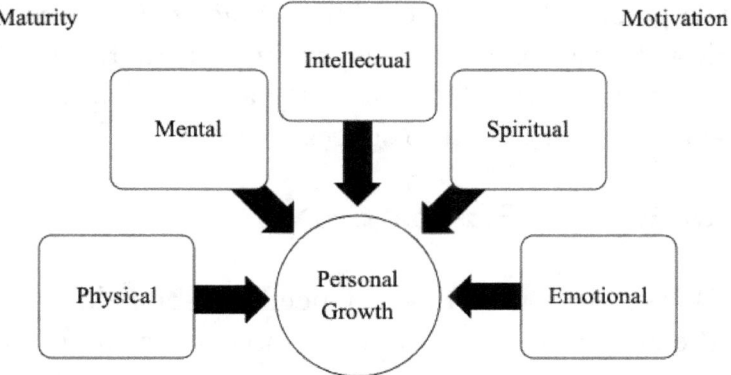

©2020 Mohammed R. Ahmed

The human body goes through the natural growth process and the four stages of life. Individual motivation sets the rate and level at which mental, emotional, intellectual, and spiritual growth are combined to achieve personal growth.

Why Should We Seek Personal Growth?

Growth is essential for the survival of human beings on earth. During the Stone Age, people lit fires using stones and friction. They hunted and cooked their food over a fire. If our ancestors were not motivated and did not use their minds, we would still live in rough-hewn huts, hunting and cooking food over a fire. Today, we live in air-conditioned houses, ride bullet trains, fly onboard supersonic jets, and use reusable rockets and capsules for space travel. These are a few good examples of outputs by people who worked hard and sought personal growth to contribute to society. An individual's personal growth leads to professional development, which, in turn, paves the way for society's growth. The combined effort of individuals and businesses to pursue growth benefits the community. Personal growth distinguishes an individual from others in the workplace and society. It also helps fulfill a person's purpose in life, increases his/her confidence and ability to guide others, fosters knowledge sharing, and makes possible the attainment of a happy life. Furthermore, during your life journey, you feel like you have accomplished your goals and are on the road to success.

How Do We Seek Personal Growth?

To seek personal growth, you need to set a life purpose. Nevertheless, goal setting alone is not sufficient to achieve personal growth. Mind, motivation, and energy are critical in achieving personal growth. The mind is the most powerful feature that an individual possesses. You must develop a growth mindset because personal growth continuously evolves and entails constant learning. It continues to grow because the environment surrounding it is also changing rapidly. Understanding the hierarchy of learning will help develop a growth mindset. The first step in the hierarchy of learning is to learn to survive, the second is to learn to benefit, and the third is to learn to grow. The first step involves motivating yourself to gain the knowledge, abilities, and capabilities needed for personal and professional success. The second step consists of motivating yourself to explore learning opportunities to gain monetary benefits. The third step is motivating yourself to undertake continuous growth to gain and share knowledge, achieve your goals in life, and fulfill your life's purpose. You must motivate yourself and develop abilities and capabilities through education and training to climb the career ladder and prosper. Individuals who focus on learning for growth believe in continuous learning and successfully achieve their personal and monetary aims. The following are 10 points that will help in generating personal growth:

1. Set a life purpose.
2. Develop a growth mindset.
3. Learn to self-motivate.
4. Improve your skills.
5. Practice continuous learning.
6. Think before you act.
7. Be truthful to yourself.
8. Learn to trust yourself.
9. Manage time and energy.
10. Remember that life is a journey.

Thinking before acting is a rational approach to achieving personal growth. Anything you do in life involves risk and the use of energy. Mental, emotional, and intellectual development enable individuals to minimize risks in decision-making and increase the chances of positive outcomes for personal growth. Truthfulness and trust are also essential in seeking personal growth, while spiritual growth will help individuals become truthful and trusting themselves. These characteristics are necessary to improve one's skills in seeking personal growth. One must remember that life goes through four phases, and every journey has a beginning and an end. As we go through the phases of life, the time and energy needed to complete our tasks will change constantly. Management of time and energy will help in seeking personal growth. Therefore, we must utilize every precious moment of our lives to accomplish our goals before reaching the end of our journey. Achieving personal growth is essential for success in life, but it is a continuous process that requires energy. Managing emotions saves energy and leads to positive outcomes. In the next chapter, let's look at anger and jealousy, which consume high energy and lead to negative outcomes.

EMOTIONS

Positive emotions can help you accomplish dreams or fall in love with someone. Negative emotions lead to the road of destruction. Learn to manage emotions and save energy to build a beautiful life.

Humans experience several emotions, which include fear, anger, sadness, jealousy, and others. Anger and jealousy are the two emotions that consume a lot of our energy and become obstacles to individual success. Everyone experiences anger, but the outcome depends on the amount and intensity of the energy used to express it. The results of expressing anger vary according to how a person develops his or her ability to manage feelings. A moderate amount of anger is normal, providing an opportunity to release excess energy, as needed, for neutral or positive outcomes.

Every individual has differing levels of energy and capabilities to manage emotions. Anger must be regulated because it is an intense feeling or will result in negative outcomes. The energy used in expressing anger, which has harmful results, could be used to generate synergy in intelligence, referred to as emotional intelligence. Managing anger is smart since it saves energy, which can be used to accomplish personal and professional goals in your life.

I like to learn from observing and interacting with people. As I mentioned earlier, I attended a management conference in a metropolitan city and encountered a panhandler who asked me if I could spare a couple of dollars. I hurriedly told him, "I'm sorry, I don't have any money." As soon as I passed him, I heard him voice his anger at me loudly. I ignored the panhandler and enjoyed an excellent presentation at the conference. I love helping people and contributing to charity. This incident made me think particularly because one of the discussions at the conference was about managing emotions.

The immediate question is why the panhandler got angry at me. A rational explanation is he was angry because his expectations failed to materialize. He believed he would get money from conference attendees as they had money to spare. I refused to give him anything, so his hopes were frustrated. This incident shows that anger absorbs an extraordinary amount of energy and results in negative outcomes. I believe someone reported his anger toward conference attendees, and he was escorted out of the convention center area since I had not seen the panhandler for the next two days. The panhandler was not able to materialize his expectations.

This incident raises the more general question of why individuals get angry. The most common reasons people get angry are because they:

1. Have unrealistic expectations
2. Desire to control others
3. Are jealous of others
4. Have a low tolerance level
5. Afraid or feel powerless
6. Inability to process triggers

The six factors influence how one uses energy and intensity to achieve outcomes. The following exhibit shows the process that results in a negative outcome, anger.

Exhibit-4: Trigger Processing

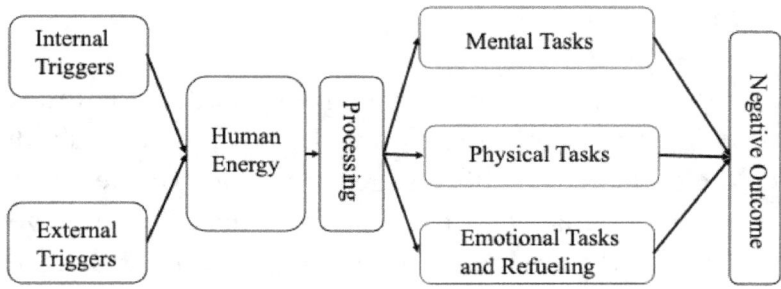

©2016 Mohammed R. Ahmed

The internal, external, or both triggers initiate energy use, the process is determined, and tasks are selected to arrive at the outcome. Let's look at the situation of John and Mike, who were playing with toys, and Harry was watching them. Suddenly, Harry approached John and took the toy from John, and John started crying. A few minutes later, Harry went to Mike and tried to grab the toy from him, and Mike got mad, pushed him to the ground, and hit him with the toy. The triggers were the same, but the two processed it differently and used energy for the different tasks to arrive at the outcome.

Anger is most likely a learned behavior. As an individual grows up, he or she learns about anger from friends, parents, and family members. The following are a few situations in which an individual may have learned anger from friends, parents, family members, and surroundings.

- If an individual is surrounded by angry and controlling friends and family during childhood, the chances are his or her anger is a learned behavior.
- If an individual has grown up in an environment where anger is used to fulfill expectations and control others,

the chances are that he or she has a problem with anger.
- If an individual lives in fear of friends and parents and holds anger inside, he or she likely has a problem with anger.

Anger issues result from learning in childhood and early adulthood and may create problems in an individual's workplace and personal life. Anger is just one of the emotions that needs to be managed to generate synergy in intelligence. Individuals need to remember that anger will not help them solve problems, change reality, build relationships with others, and achieve control or power in their workplace.

The best way to deal with anger is to recognize the problem, identify triggers, and learn to manage anger. Anger results from an individual's interpretation of triggers and inability to manage energy for emotions. People need to be smart, not angry, and use their energy for positive outcomes. The other feeling or emotion that focuses on managing energy to succeed is jealousy.

Jealousy

We are all humans with energy and feelings or emotions. We learn how to use our energy to express our feelings or emotions. Envy and jealousy are often thought of as two emotions generated when a child's mind starts recognizing needs for survival, safety, love, and pleasure. As we grow up and enter the workplace, jealousy becomes part of our professional relationships with others. There is a difference between envy and jealousy, but researchers and individuals sometimes use these two interchangeably. The difference between envy and jealousy is the energy level used to express the feeling or emotion; in other words, both are simply different levels of the same emotion.

Learning from observation

I believe that we can learn from the observation of individuals and groups about how envy and jealousy can become harmful if an individual's emotions are not managed. This idea can become clear by examining the case of three children named John, Kasey, and Robert. They are friends, attend the same school, and are in the same grade. They often play together after school. One day, John brings a new electronic handheld game to play with his friends Kasey and Robert after school. Kasey plays the game and says, "I love this game, and I wish I had this game at my house to play." Robert responds to his friends that he likes the game, but at his house, he has a game that is better than John's new game. They are taking turns playing the game, and it seems they enjoy themselves. However, during the third turn, Robert drops the game on the floor, breaking it into pieces. At that point, everyone looks at each other. In this example, Kasey's response to his friends suggests that his emotions lead to envy and Robert's jealousy. Robert's response to his friends, saying that his game is better than John's new game, expresses a negative emotion. Robert's jealousy may have generated repressed anger, and the game may have slipped out of his hand because of the emotion coming to the surface, or the anger may have led him to drop the game on the floor intentionally.

The lesson from the above example is that envy and jealousy are part of the same emotion, and if they are not managed, they will consume a large amount of energy for a negative outcome. The following exhibit shows three levels of jealousy and energy consumption.

Exhibit-5: Three Levels of Jealousy

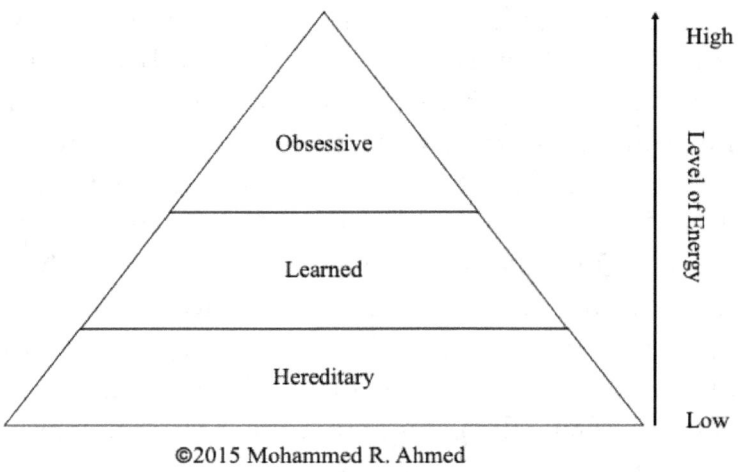

©2015 Mohammed R. Ahmed

The first level of jealousy could be hereditary. It likely exists in all human beings. The second level of jealousy generates anger and possibly leads to negative outcomes. At this level, a learned jealousy may be acquired from family, friends, and the surrounding environment. The third level of jealousy is obsessive jealousy. It is an obsessive form of jealousy because of individual deficiencies. The individual deficiencies include unrealistic fears, low self-esteem, and other insecurities. Obsessive jealousy involves frequent anger directed at others, as expressed in efforts to control or lie about others.

It is important to remember that we are human beings and will take what we have learned from our personal lives into our work lives. If we learn to manage our emotions early, we will likely successfully prevent jealousy from leading to a negative outcome in professional life.

Sources of Jealousy

We need to identify what triggers jealousy and learn to manage our emotions so that they do not progress into anger and consume energy that results in a negative outcome. The most common source of jealousy arises out of the fear of losing a relationship or of not having a specific relationship to begin with. We are human beings, and we have personal and professional relationships. Various relationships exist between family members, friends, and coworkers, and jealousy comes into play differently.

Jealousy exists among family, friends, groups, teams, organizations, and nations. Money can cause jealousy in personal relationships and work life. A lack of positive workplace relationships between certain people in an organization usually leads to jealousy. Monetary compensation for assigned work perceived as unjust can create jealousy in the workplace. Varying levels of knowledge among people performing the same tasks can create jealousy in the workplace. Jealousy has existed since early civilization, and it will continue to exist in the future. We should be most concerned about obsessive-jealous people because they create obstacles to achieving our goals. Understanding emotions such as anger and jealousy and sources will help individuals manage their energy and use it to achieve success in areas that result in positive outcomes. Managing emotions leads to rational decisions and lowers the consumption of energy. Rational decisions will not result in positive outcomes without building trust in yourself and trust with others. Next, we will review how to build trust and trust or not to trust.

TRUST

Trust builds confidence between parties and reduces uncertainty. It takes the energy of two to build trust, which can be easily broken by one untrustworthy action.

We live in an uncertain world, but trust is needed to live a normal life and conduct everyday individual tasks. This doesn't mean that we trust everyone in the world, or even everything that we see, feel, or touch. This explains why we are constantly faced with the decision to trust or not to trust. When you are in an uncertain world, and the concern about trust consumes your energy, building trust reduces energy consumption. The word "trust" is sometimes misunderstood and may have several definitions. You cannot trust anyone until you build trust with them. Trust is built between parties, and assuming trust exists exhausts emotional energy. The simple explanation of trust is a behavior structured around emotional, physical, spiritual, economic, and social satisfaction. This behavior involves emotions, and emotions use human energy.

Trust is important in personal, professional, and social life. A lack of trust creates conflict, leading to negative emotions and energy loss. If we understand the hierarchy of trust, it may be easier to decide whether to trust. The following exhibit shows the progression of trust.

Exhibit-6: Progression of Trust

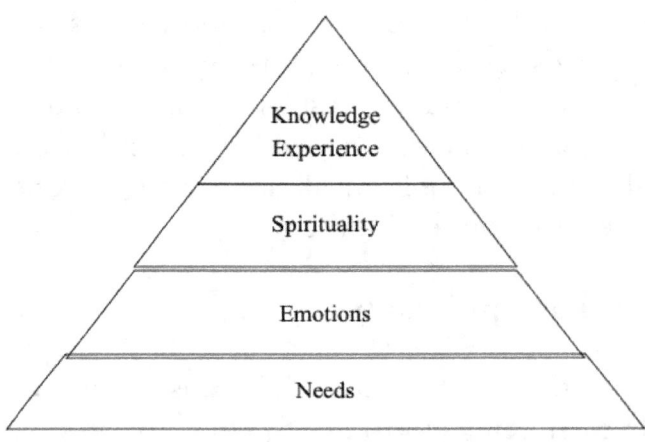

©2016 Mohammed R. Ahmed

Trust is a learning process that begins as soon as we are born. Just imagine that you are holding a two- or three-month-old baby. The baby starts crying. You try your best to comfort the baby, but the baby won't stop crying. Then, as soon as the mother takes the baby from your arms, she stops crying in her trusted hands. Babies learn to trust their mothers because they are confident, they will satisfy their needs. This is an example of the first learning experience of trust-building based on needs such as food, comfort, love, and safety. As we grow older, some of our needs will change, and the number of needs will increase. Still, we will continue to trust others based on our needs. As we get older and become more dependent on others, we once again start trusting others based on more primary needs, just as babies trust their mothers.

Trust Based on Emotions

As we grow older and hone our abilities to understand our emotions, we also begin trusting based on our emotions. Do you remember first meeting a girl or boy you liked? You may remember that you started trusting him or her and may have wanted to spend the rest of your life with that person. This was a trust based on emotions. Emotional trust arises from emotional needs, and rational thinking is sometimes absent. Trust based on emotions results from certain emotional experiences, attachments, dependency, and variability in emotional control. People of all ages use emotions to build trust and benefit from each other.

Trust Based on Spirituality

Spirituality-based trust is unique because it is not trust in another human being, a group of people, or an organization. It is the trust between an invisible, powerful, and intangible entity. This trust is unquestionable and requires no prior experience, knowledge, or empirical evidence to be built. For example, imagine you trust a friend to help you prepare for an exam, but your friend doesn't help you. You will then question the trustworthiness of your friend. However, imagine you were spiritually prepared and expected to pass the exam but failed it. You would not question your spiritual trust but seek a rational explanation to maintain its strength. This is why spiritual trust becomes the foundation for building self-trust. It also generates positive emotions and helps individuals refuel their energy.

Trust Based on Knowledge and Experience

If you trust your doctor, you do so because of his or her knowledge and experience. If you are in a classroom and interested in learning, you are doing so because you trust the instructor or professor based on his or her knowledge and experience. The result from trusting the doctor may lead to good health, and trusting the professor may lead to gaining the knowledge needed to succeed in the workplace or elsewhere. The kind of trust between doctors and patients and professors and learners is based on information regarding the knowledge and experience of the parties involved in the trust-based relationship, and this type of trust benefits both parties. We build trust based on another person's knowledge and experience and use our knowledge and experience to trust others.

To Trust or Not to Trust?

Whether to trust is sometimes difficult because of our changing environments and lack of information to make certain decisions. If significant information is available and we have already had a positive experience with an individual, group, or institution, it is easier to make the decision to trust. For example, it is often easy for people to make decisions to trust politicians based on information regarding past experiences of broken promises.

The following is a list of ten things that may help you when deciding to trust and minimize the use of energy:

1. Trust is a behavior that shows your level of confidence in others.
2. Trust involves two or more responsive participants.
3. Trust is built if two parties have the same confidence level in each other.
4. Trust is built on information, knowledge, or experience that can easily be established.
5. Trust based on needs is a one-way trust and can be easily violated by others.
6. Trust that is based on economics is always short-term trust.
7. Trust is difficult to establish with addiction because they

often abuse the trust of others.
8. Trust is difficult to establish based on individual emotions.
9. The foundation of self-trust is spiritual trust.
10. Trust can always be manipulated if one party changes its mind about the relationship.

Trust brings stability to our lives, and its misuse leads to emotional, physical, economic, and social instability. Uncertainty in determining whether to trust or not to raise energy consumption. Therefore, we must ask ourselves whether we should trust others before trusting them and making decisions, not allowing the uncertainty to prolong and consume our energy.

I attended a management conference and had an opportunity to participate in a session on trust and spirituality at the workplace. During the meeting, we were split into small groups to discuss trust between management and employees, self-trust, and spirituality at the workplace. I tried to break the silence in our group by sharing the belief that the first step in building trust is to be truthful to oneself. I further emphasized that spirituality in the workplace creates an environment for people to be honest with themselves. There was a pause for a moment in the group because of the realization that being untruthful means lying to yourself. We do not like to think we could lie to ourselves because we believe lying occurs between two or more people. The fact is that lying happens between us and the people around us in all aspects of our lives. The chances are each one of us may have lied about something in our lives. Lying is sharing an untruthful statement with others, hoping they will believe it as the truth. Being untruthful to yourself is like telling everyone that you are dry when everyone can see that you are standing in the rain and you are wet. As individuals and as a society, we need to be concerned about lying because it affects our personal and professional lives, and it constantly consumes our energy because of the fear that someone will find out the truth.

We learn to be untruthful as we grow up through our interactions with family and friends. If we were to develop the fear of telling the truth early because of punishment or sharing untruth because of punishment or a reward, it would become the foundation for being untruthful to ourselves and others. Fear is an emotion and consumes a lot of individual energy. I have heard several stories about how childhood experiences influenced people to be untruthful to themselves in their adult life.

I cannot forget one story of a childhood experience I heard from an adult decades ago because it included four of the five motivating factors for being untruthful. During his/her childhood, the adult was introduced to untruth by the controlling and disciplining parent. This was a powerful experience for the child because the child was pleasing the parent out of fear. The story's lesson is that we learn to be untruthful as a child or an adult due to our environment. When you are untruthful, fear and anxiety consume a large amount of energy, and it will impact other areas of your life when you need the energy to succeed. The five primary reasons that motivate people to be untruthful are called the 5 Ps: (1) please, (2) protect, (3) provoke, (4) profit, and (5) pleasure.

The best way to manage your energy, build trust, and be truthful is to avoid people who lie to provoke, make money, or satisfy their psychological needs. If someone is lying to you, do not spend your energy on getting mad at them, but you should understand the motivation behind their lies and take steps to protect yourself from them in your personal and professional life. If you are untruthful to yourself, it means you cannot trust yourself. If you cannot trust yourself, you cannot be trusted by others, and you will have a bumpy road to success. Trust brings responsibility, which is critical for building trust. Next, we will review the types of responsibilities and responsibilities for actions and outcomes.

RESPONSIBILITY

Responsibility leads to accountability and rewards or consequences for your actions. It reduces the chances of negative outcomes and the use of energy.

We have personal and professional responsibilities, and energy is required to accomplish tasks involved in fulfilling them. Responsible, reliable, and trustworthy people understand the importance of meeting their obligations and fulfilling their promises. The following exhibits show the three types of responsibilities we generally encounter.

Exhibit-7: Types of Responsibility

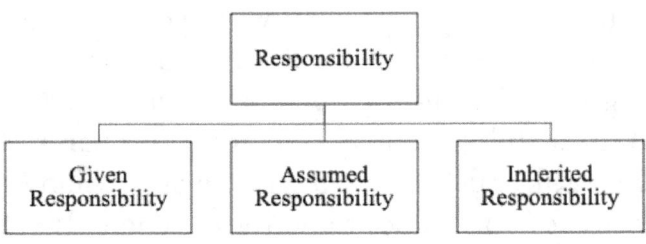

©2015 Mohammed R. Ahmed

Responsible people proactively identify and address problems and ensure they do not harm or inconvenience others. In doing so, they reduce the chances of negative outcomes and thus reduce the waste of energy.

A given (explicitly allocated) responsibility is when your parents ask you to watch your little sibling for a few minutes, and you accept the responsibility given to you by your parents. An assumed responsibility is asking your parents for a pet rabbit for your birthday. Your parents warned you it would come with great responsibility because you must feed, clean, and care for a rabbit. You insisted to your parents that you would take care of the rabbit, and as a result, you received the gift and took on the inherited responsibility. People who take on assumed, inherited, or given (explicitly allocated) responsibility to accomplish a task or achieve broader goals or outcomes understand the importance of responsibility and individual energy management. They take responsibility for both their actions and the outcomes, whether these actions are positive or negative. Accepting the negative outcome as a fact reduces energy consumption and refuels the energy to accomplish the next tasks. One must learn to be responsible personally and professionally to succeed in life.

Responsibility for Actions and Outcomes

Suppose that you were playing with your sibling in your backyard. You pushed your sibling for fun, and your sibling fell to the ground and got hurt. Your parents asked you what happened. As a child, you may have told your parents that you were sorry for pushing her and were willing to take responsibility for your actions and the outcome. If you instead said that she slipped and fell on her own or that you did not know how she fell to the ground, you did not take responsibility for your actions or their outcome. This may seem like childish behavior that often occurs while growing up, and you may think that children may grow out of this behavior as they age. However, the family is a space for learning about appropriate behavior, and parents create an environment where children can learn how to be responsible for their actions. In a family space where punishment occurs because of negative outcomes, children may not learn to be responsible for their actions because of their fear of punishment.

Responsible behavior is critical for success in both personal and professional life. In personal life, if parents do not take on the responsibility of raising their children, or if they do not teach them to be responsible or to take responsibility for the outcomes of their actions, the children may not learn responsible behavior. In professional life, the workplace is a space for learning responsible behavior. Managers should create an environment where employees can learn to be responsible for their tasks and actions. Otherwise, they may encounter problems with the quality of products and services in the marketplace because they are not focusing on the responsible behavior of the employees.

For example, I used to go to a globally recognized fast food chain and ask for a breakfast sandwich without meat, and I once received a sandwich with meat three times in a row. In another case, I requested a 90-day medicine supply from the pharmacy and received a 30-day supply twice instead. On a different occasion, I ordered a screen protector for my phone online and received one designed for a different phone model instead. The question is, what causes these errors in business practice? These errors result from the lack of responsible behavior by the people providing customer service. Such a lack of responsibility impacts the quality of products or services delivered and the competitive advantage of a company in the marketplace.

The following are a few examples where energy is not used for successful outcomes because of the lack of understanding of responsibility.

1. John and Julie blame their young children for wasting their hard work in raising them because instead of being

able to finish college, the children end up having more problems in both their personal and work lives.
2. Jamie is upset because her husband throws soda cans in regular trash rather than in the recycle bin.
3. Jean bumps a parked car by opening her car door in the parking lot. No one was in the parking lot, so she left without saying anything to anyone.
4. Joan is frustrated with employees in her department because they call her whenever a customer has any questions. She told them not to call her anymore and to resolve the customer's problems independently.
5. Jerry loves drinking and dancing on the weekends, and he always invites friends unwilling to drink and drive to ride with him to the clubs.

If we understand our given, assumed, and inherited responsibilities, we can prepare and plan to fulfill them. Fulfilling the responsibilities requires energy, which will result in positive outcomes. On the other hand, energy is used for negative outcomes without fulfilling responsibilities. In the above example, Jamie wastes her energy and gets upset whenever she finds cans in the regular bins due to her husband's irresponsible behavior. One of the reasons individuals and groups do not take responsibility is because they are not aware of the consequences and the energy loss that occurs when someone doesn't take responsibility. Everyone needs to learn to manage their energy and use it for tasks that result in positive outcomes. Furthermore, we must understand that there are consequences for our actions and sometimes consequences for people around us.

Actions and Consequences

Everyone should be concerned about consequences because we operate businesses and conduct our personal lives in an uncertain environment. Consequences, or outcomes, result from our decisions and actions. We make hundreds of choices in our personal and professional lives and take actions that may result in consequences or rewards. Safety, survival, financial, emotional, and legal consequences should be of utmost concern for individuals, families, and businesses because they may result in difficult circumstances. For example, if individuals are late for work, they must decide whether to break the speed limit or inform their workplace that they will be late. The decision to break the speed results in high energy consumption and may result in negative outcomes if they become involved in an accident or stopped by police.

Work and family settings are complex environments because there is constant interaction between two or more parties concerned with the consequences of people's actions. There are three types of decision-makers in work and family settings: rational, irrational, and reward seekers. When an individual puts a decision into action, they are responsible for its consequences. Informed, rational individuals take full responsibility for their actions. When deciding, a rational individual will evaluate the risk involved and if it is acceptable, and then they will put the decision into action. Irrational individuals are not responsible for their decisions and actions and may be unaware of the risk involved. They may be willing to take risks regardless of the consequences.

Exhibit-8 Actions and Consequences

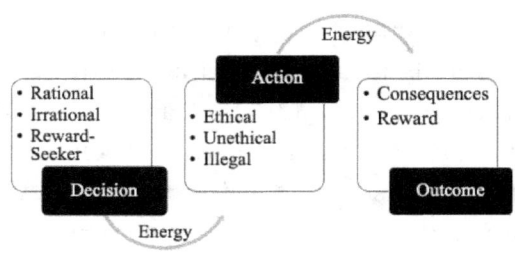

©2017 Mohammed R. Ahmed

A reward seeker takes the risk to receive a reward. An individual is only concerned about the rewards and will do anything to achieve them. Businesses and individuals operate in an uncertain environment, so it is important to evaluate the consequences of a decision before making it. Risk tolerance should also be considered when making decisions. An explanation or justification after experiencing the consequences will not change the outcome. At the same time, individuals should not fear consequences and make rational decisions. Individuals can be rational, irrational, or reward-seeking when making decisions, acting on them, and facing consequences. Being rational saves energy because it minimizes risk in decision-making and negative outcomes. Negative outcomes bring anger and anxiety, absorb more energy, and impact future personal and professional tasks. Being responsible and rational in today's dynamic environment requires continuous learning. Understanding the learning process in the next chapter will help gain knowledge to succeed.

LEARNING

Learning is a natural process of gaining knowledge that requires energy. As children, it thrills us, and as adults, we make it a choice.

We start learning as soon as we are born. We learn to talk, walk, express ourselves, and interact, all of which require energy. As we grow up, we learn to ride, swim, drive, and so on. In the early part of our lives, the family guides us on what to learn and what not to learn. They indirectly manage our energy by controlling our activities.

As we age, we decide what to learn, what not to learn, and how much to learn. We will succeed if we understand what we should learn and the learning process. There are three things about the learning process.

1. Learning is a progressive process.
2. Learning is a continuous process.
3. Learning is a hierarchical process.

Learning is a progressive process because we have to go through a few sequential and/or parallel steps to accomplish something. To ride a bicycle, first, we need to learn how to balance on two wheels; next, we learn to pedal, maintain speed, use brakes to avoid a crash, and so on.

Learning is a continuous process because the environment surrounding us is constantly changing. We have to learn new ways to accomplish the same old tasks or learn new tasks that will become part of our lives. We communicated by mailing handwritten, typewritten, and word processor-composed letters. Now, we use email. We used to stay in touch with family and friends by mail and telephone. Now, we use social networking and texting to stay in touch with them.

Learning is a hierarchical process because individuals decide whether to climb the hierarchy of learning, that is, to learn to survive, benefit, grow, and achieve a certain level of growth. The decision results from the individual's motivation to learn or relearn and how much energy will be spent on learning. The following is an exhibit of the hierarchy of learning.

Exhibit-9: Hierarchy of Learning

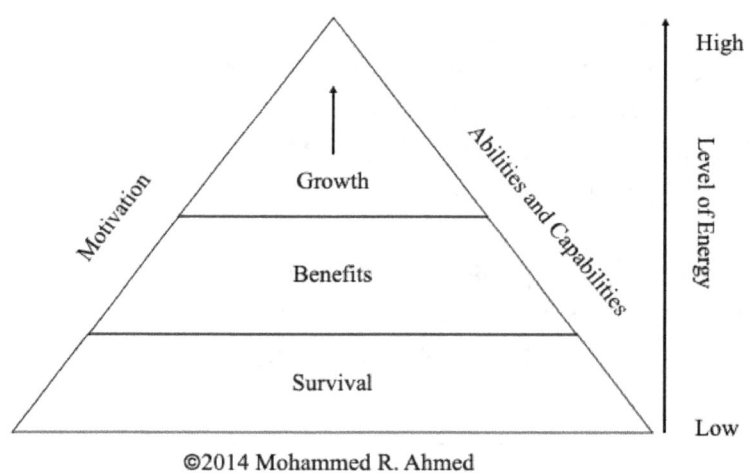

©2014 Mohammed R. Ahmed

The decision to learn for survival, benefits, or growth depends on the individual's motivation in the workplace. Success at each step depends on the individual's ability to recognize learning needs and capability to learn or relearn. The hierarchy of learning exists in both personal and professional life.

Individual Motivation Leads to a Learning Hierarchy

Danny, Jerry, and Suzy, high school friends who turned 16, started working part-time for a local retail store chain, bagging merchandise and helping customers. They were motivated to work for the company because it paid above the minimum wage and had a promotion policy within the company. After graduating high school, they all decided to stay with the retail chain to explore career opportunities.

Danny had two years of experience with front-end service—bagging merchandise and helping customers. He applied for a full-time, front-end service position at the store and got hired by the company. He was motivated to work as a front-end service person, could recognize what he needed to learn for the position, and could deliver customer service. He settled down with a full-time position as a front-end service person.

While working part-time at the front-end service, Jerry networked with the stock clerks and the warehouse department manager because he was motivated by the advancement opportunities in the warehouse department and the difference in salaries and bonuses. He learned what he needed to learn to be a stock clerk and prepared himself for the position. He applied for that position and got hired by the company in the warehouse department.

Suzy was interested in the retail store business and learned about the management opportunities. She decided to continue working part-time as a customer service representative. She applied for the part-time customer service representative position and got hired by the company. Suzy decided to work part-time to attend the local college, get her bachelor's degree in business administration, and explore management opportunities at the company.

The three young individuals decided where they would be on the level of the learning hierarchy based on individual motivation, abilities, and capabilities. After four years with the company, Danny still happily works as a front-end service person. Jerry has become a warehouse department assistant manager and has received several pay raises. Suzy graduated with her bachelor's degree and was hired as the retail store manager. This is an example of how individual motivation and the amount of energy an individual is willing to use leads to a learning hierarchy, and the level of success in the growth stage depends on the individual's ability to recognize the learning needs and capabilities of the individual.

In the knowledge-based economy, individual self-motivation is not enough to create value for the company. You need to find organizations that motivate employees, identify their learning needs, and develop their abilities and capabilities to generate personal and professional growth. Learning leads to creativity and dreams of something new or large. We will discuss the dreams in the next chapter.

DREAMS

Dreams are imaginations that can be turned into reality with individual motivation and positive energy.

The word "dream" often refers to creative goals that individuals are eager to accomplish and require great energy. When a dream materializes, it changes one's life. Thomas Edison, Mahatma Gandhi, President John F. Kennedy, Dr. Martin Luther King, and Nelson Mandela had dreams, showing that the world could improve through their materialization. Thomas Edison was successful in lighting up the world, Mahatma Gandhi worked toward ending the British rule of India, President Kennedy initiated the process whereby humans became capable of walking on the moon, Dr. Martin Luther King was able to bring justice to a society plagued by racial inequality, and Nelson Mandela brought peace and racial equality to Africa. All successful scientists and leaders have dreams, and they encourage everyone else to have their own to challenge the status quo. Dreams allow individuals to think deeply and creatively and to work hard to accomplish their goals.

A dream is like setting a goal in the subconscious mind so that the conscious mind can accomplish it. Every individual has a dream, which can be materialized by formulating and implementing specific strategies using the conscious mind. Businesses understand that an individual's dream is the driving force for personal and professional growth. As a result, several businesses, including technology companies, have transformed the workplace into a campus-like environment, providing additional time and comfortable environments for employees to pursue their dreams. The businesses where employees have a chance to dream will be more creative in developing products and delivering services to their customers.

A dream is a goal based on positive emotions in the subconscious mind, and it can be accomplished by transposing the positive emotions into the conscious mind to formulate a practical strategy to materialize the dream. Everyone there may have once thought of an idea to solve a problem or develop a product or service and soon realized that somebody was already marketing that solution, product, or service on television or the Internet. The reason an individual's dream may not materialize. In contrast, someone else can market the same idea on television because the individual did not put the right positive emotions into the strategy formulation and implementation to achieve the goals.

Exhibit-10: Dreams

©2017 Mohammed R. Ahmed

The above model suggests that to materialize a dream, you must transpose positive emotions into the strategy and its implementation. Otherwise, it will be a very different kind of dream, more like the one we have when sleeping. In other words, a difference exists between having a dream for accomplishing something and dreaming while asleep.

Dreaming During Sleep

The dreams that occur during sleep are of random images, audio, video, and feelings related to what had occurred during the day, week, or months before the period of sleep. They are usually created by an individual's imagination. For example, a child who watches a monster movie during the day may dream about the monster during sleep, along with any other event experienced during the day. Such a dream is an imaginary experience, and it will not materialize. It may be a random image or video from the past stored in the child's subconscious mind, or it may be the result of the complicated processes of the imagination and emotions of the child who reconstructed a monster video during sleep.

Exhibit-11: Dreaming

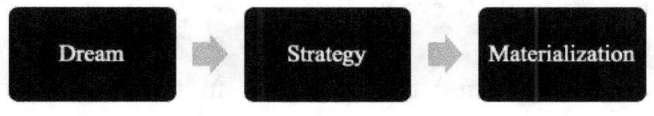

©2017 Mohammed R. Ahmed

The above model suggests that dreaming starts in the individual space where images, audio, and videos are created. The triggering event activates emotions, and the emotional energy is utilized based on the imagination to construct (act) the dream.

I believe in learning through interaction and observation. Using this approach in both the classroom and the workplace, I have learned that three types of emotions are involved in the dreams we have during sleep about the workplace.

1 Positive emotion
2. Neutral emotion
3. Negative emotion

Positive Emotional Energy:

Individuals with positive emotions may leave work but are still emotionally attached to it because they want to advance in the workplace. They may dream at random, and they often dream about the workplace.

Example of a Dream:

I had a dream that my company would expand its operations to China, and I was asked to lead its Chinese operations starting in June. I was glad that the job was right after my graduation.

Neutral Emotional Energy:

An individual with neutral emotions in the workplace leaves work without thinking about it until he or she returns. They may dream at random, but they rarely dream about work.

Example of a Dream:

I had a dream that the company would spin off a wireless division and ask for volunteers from the fiber optics division to join the new venture. I thought they already had enough volunteers, and I did not feel pressured to join the spin-off division.

Negative Emotional Energy:

An individual with negative emotions leaves the workplace but is emotionally attached to the work because he or she is unhappy with the occupational situation. They may dream at random, and they dream about work.

Example of a Dream:

I dreamed I won the lottery and returned to work the next day. As soon as my supervisor started his same morning routine of complaining about my work, I told the manager that I was quitting, and I left the job.

These three examples of dreams while sleeping have no direct connection to reality because the experience results from the individual imagination, and such dreams are generally about something an individual is interested in doing. In the dream resulting from positive emotions, the individual was interested in professional growth opportunities and the managerial position. The individual with the neutral emotions was happy with the status quo and did not use much imagination to construct the experience, having random images of the workplace in the dream and not bothering to recall anything more significant. The individual with negative emotions was unhappy with the workplace and interested in quitting. The imagination led to a scenario where the lottery was won to facilitate quitting.

The lesson we need to remember both in our personal and professional lives is that dreams lead to creative ideas and positive emotional energy is needed to materialize a dream. Dreams in sleep result from an individual's imagination, distinct from reality. Research and individual experience show that everyone dreams in sleep, but few people remember the dreams, and few do not. Materializing dreams requires intelligence, and we will learn how to generate synergy in intelligence in the next chapter.

INTELLIGENCE

Everyone processes abilities and capabilities to learn and apply the knowledge needed to succeed. Intelligent people think critically and learn continuously.

Intelligence can be described as learning and using knowledge and skills to solve a problem, resolve a situation, or benefit from an opportunity. It involves logical data and knowledge-based reasoning to make rational decisions or achieve positive outcomes. It involves mental, emotional, and physical tasks, and all the tasks require energy. If we manage our energy, we can increase our intelligence, which in turn increases the number of positive outcomes in our lives. It means you will be able to ride on the road of success. An individual's total intelligence has several components. The following exhibit shows the total intelligence quotient and the three intelligence variables over time.

Exhibit-12: Total Intelligence Quotient

$$TIQ = IQ + EQ + UQ$$

©2016 Mohammed R. Ahmed

The level of intelligence is measured by its quotient. The total intelligence quotient (TIQ) is a function of the intelligence quotient (IQ), emotional quotient (EQ), and unknown quotient (UQ).

Everyone worldwide understands IQ measurement, but EQ is

not recognized because some researchers believe it can be measured, and some don't agree with the measurement process. Every human has emotions and uses emotional energy, which needs measurement. EQ is the synergy generated by feeling and managing emotions, and several unknown quotients make up the total intelligence quotient.

Human energy management and emotional intelligence probably existed since humans started life on Earth. Every parent may have witnessed energy use and emotional intelligence at work while a child was growing up and may have used some other label or word to explain the child's emotional intelligence. The best way to understand emotional Intelligence is to listen to people, observe their behaviors, and feel their emotions.

What makes our personal or professional lives good, bad, or miserable depends upon how we use our energy to act and behave in our personal, professional, and social lives. We are usually taught these skills by our parents as we grow up, and we teach our children while we raise them. For example, when I was a little boy, I pinched my cousin because she was not sharing the toys with me, but she started crying when I pinched her. My uncle observed us and asked me to go and sit with him. After I sat down and started complaining about my cousin, he softly pinched me. I felt the pinch and told him it hurt. He said, "Yes, pinching hurts people. That's why you should not pinch your cousin." Afterward, he instructed me to ask my cousin to share the toys with me politely. He also asked my cousin to listen to my request for her to share the toys. My uncle taught us to use energy for a positive outcome by asking me to be polite and my cousin to listen to my requests. She agreed to my polite request, and we played together happily. Growing up and playing with my cousins may have been easy, but working with grownups is not easy.

In addition to learning from our parents, we learn how to use our energy to act and behave based on our interactions with family members, friends, teachers, coworkers, and managers. As we go through our lifecycles, we forget how to feel, observe, and listen, particularly in our personal and professional lives. We separate our home lives and work lives. There is nothing wrong with separating our personal and professional lives, but both parts of our lives require interactions with human beings with emotions, which require energy. We spend approximately one-third of our lives with our families, one-third with our work families, and one-third sleeping. Therefore, to be successful in any environment where interaction with human beings is necessary, we need to learn to feel emotions, observe behavior, and listen to what others say. If we learn these three skills, we will save energy and use emotional intelligence to succeed in the workplace and our lives.

What is Emotional Intelligence

Emotional intelligence is the synergy generated by managing emotions, involving an individual's ability to regulate energy. It is an individual human process used to achieve desired performance outcomes. Therefore, emotional intelligence differs from person to person. The emotional intelligence process starts with a triggering event. Based on the processing of the trigger, individuals feel and manage their emotions to generate synergy in intelligence. Feeling and managing emotions is a process that includes abilities and capabilities and the amount and intensity of energy needed to generate synergy. The synergy in intelligence is emotional intelligence. Emotional intelligence (synergy) is used to achieve a desired outcome. There are three possible desired outcomes from using emotional intelligence: positive, neutral, or negative. The following is the model for emotional intelligence.

Exhibit-13: Emotional Intelligence Model

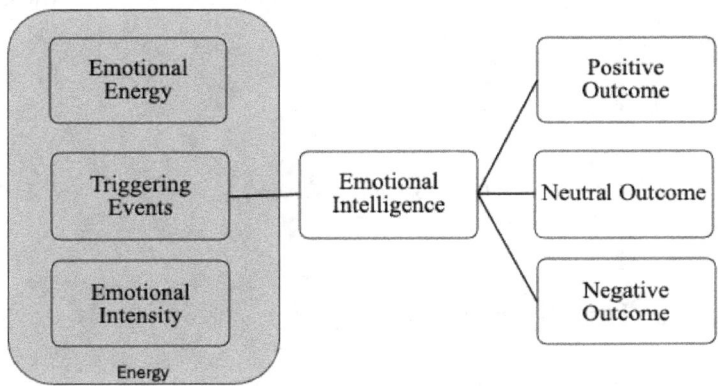

©2016 Mohammed R. Ahmed

Achieving the desired outcome depends on how well individuals manage and understand others' emotions. Managing emotions involves analyzing and controlling the internal and external emotional triggers, regulating the intensity of the emotions resulting from the trigger, and using the appropriate amount of emotional energy. Everyone has these abilities and capabilities, and they go through this emotion management process on a conscious and unconscious level. The following exhibit highlights emotional intelligence and the possible outcomes resulting from individual abilities and capabilities to feel and manage emotions.

Exhibit-14: Emotional Intelligence Model

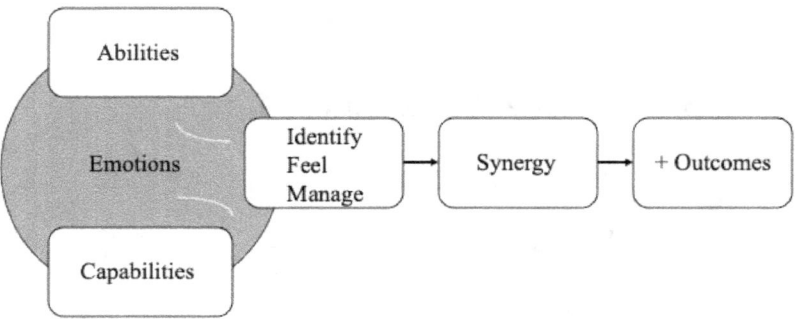

©2016 Mohammed R. Ahmed

Emotional Intelligence at Work

Emotions exist in every living being. Human beings have a good sense of expressing and sensing these emotions. Emotional intelligence starts developing as soon as the child is born, and the best way to understand it is by observing children.

Three triplets sleep in separate cribs in a children's room while their mother rests in another room.

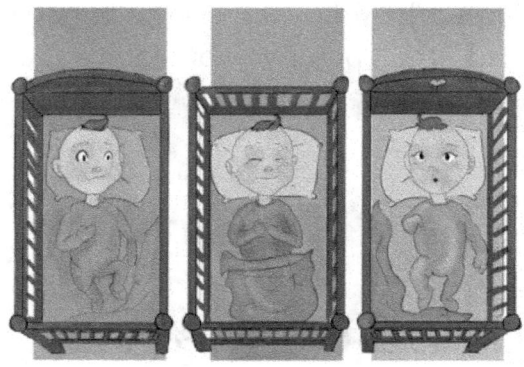

©2010 Mohammed R. Ahmed

One of the triplets wakes up and starts crying. The second triplet joins him crying, and so does the third triplet.

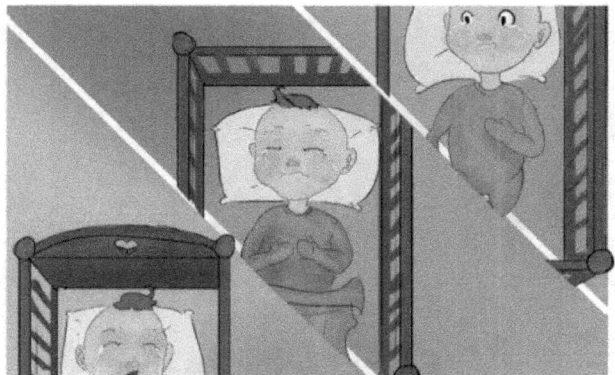

©2010 Mohammed R. Ahmed

The mother walks into the room to calm them down and then leaves to prepare milk bottles.

©2010 Mohammed R. Ahmed

The first triplet starts crying again, the second follows the first and starts whining (crying on and off), and the third triplet watches the other two brothers crying.

©2010 Mohammed R. Ahmed

This time, the triplets do not get immediate attention from the mother because she is preparing milk bottles for them.

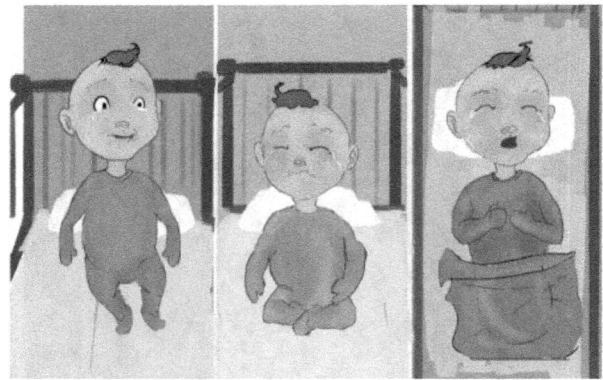

©2010 Mohammed R. Ahmed

The first triplet starts crying louder and gets emotional because he does not get immediate attention from his mother. To find her, he climbs the crib (which he has never done before) and falls on the cushioned floor. The second triplet stands on the crib and watches the brother on the floor. The third triplet watches the brother on the floor while lying in his crib.

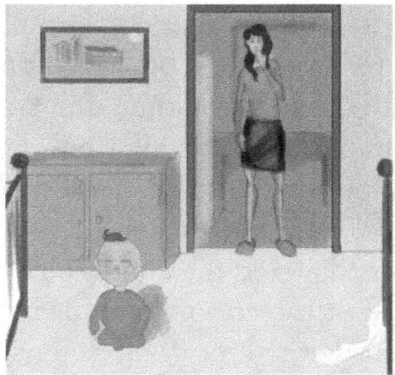

©2010 Mohammed R. Ahmed

In a few minutes, the mother walks into the room, surprised to find the first triplet on the floor, and immediately picks him up to check he is not hurt.

©2010 Mohammed R. Ahmed

She asks firmly, 'How did you get out of the crib, son'? The child watches the mother with his twinkling eyes, and if he could speak, he would say, 'Mother, I used my emotional intelligence.'

This is an example of how a child learns to feel and manage emotions, regulate energy, and try to achieve a desired outcome. We can learn from this example that emotional intelligence exists in all ages, genders, and races, and how and when it will be used depends on the individual. The three triplets were healthy, had the same energy, and were hungry. The first triplet, by nature, had high emotional intensity. He was hungry, started crying, and expected his mother to respond to his call. He did not receive an immediate response from his mother; it triggered the child's emotional intelligence, and he climbed out of the crib to find his mother. The second appears to have moderate emotional intensity as he stood up on the crib crying, and the third triplet seems to have low emotional intensity as he was lying in the crib crying for his mother. If we can measure the individual's emotional intelligence and understand how to match it with the given situation, we can improve individual performance.

Listen, Observe, and Feel (LOF)

We can understand emotional intelligence and how it works by listening, observing, feeling, and analyzing an event. This is the best way to understand how humans learn to regulate energy and generate synergy in intelligence to achieve the desired outcome.

According to the Federal Aviation Administration (FAA), on January 15, 2009, a US Airways pilot performed an emergency landing in the Hudson River. It is believed that this was the first time an airplane had landed on the water in 45 years, and all the passengers aboard the aircraft emerged alive and well. The aircraft was hit by a bird shortly after take-off and, as a result, lost power in both engines. The aircraft captain took control of the plane to land on the river. The triggering event for the pilot was the loss of power in the aircraft's two engines.

To understand how the captain managed his emotions, you must listen to or read the conversation transcripts between the pilot and the air traffic controllers (FAA, 2009). The entire conversation lasted less than three minutes. As mentioned, listening, observing, and feeling are the best way to learn about emotional intelligence. The audio transcripts show that the pilot used low emotional intensity while communicating with the tower and employed high emotional intensity to find a safe place to land. In less than two minutes, the captain had identified possible landing options, processed them, rejected a few, and selected the safest option to land on the water. As identified earlier, emotional intelligence refers to a set of abilities and capabilities that individuals possess to feel, control, and manage emotions in achieving a desired outcome. The aircraft's captain was focused on safely landing the aircraft (desired outcome), and he utilized his abilities and capabilities to feel, control, and manage emotions to do this. The event exemplifies how matching individual emotional intelligence with the right job generates synergy to achieve a desired outcome. In this case, it was a positive outcome, with the aircraft safely landing on the Hudson River.

Let's look at another event where I was listening, observing, and feeling the emotions of a group of people. It was Saturday afternoon on Waikiki Beach in Hawaii. I needed to relax and recuperate from the previous two days of brainstorming at the annual Business conference. After a few hours of relaxation on the beach, I returned to my hotel room, got ready, and joined my family and friends for a luau. As soon I arrived at the luau, I could smell the delicious Hawaiian food, hear the melodious music, and see people in colorful outfits dancing and welcoming the guests. After we were seated at the table, I adjusted to the music and the emotions of the people surrounding me. As the evening progressed with food and drinks and the show started, the luau atmosphere changed for me. I went to the luau to enjoy food, music, and dance, but my mind started asking why some people were wearing colorful outfits to the luau and why some were shouting at the dancers, their emotions unchecked. I looked around the luau and noticed that it was packed with diverse groups of people. Some enjoyed the family outing--the food and drinks, the dancing, and the show-- and some were very loud and freely letting their emotions out. I relaxed while feeling their emotions, observing their behavior, and listening to them.

I could feel the emotional energy of a diverse group of people. The group sitting around the bar wore Hawaiian shirts and dresses, powerfully high-fiving each other, butting heads, and shouting at the dancers as if they were controlling the show. Those sitting on the left side of the stage were getting up from their chairs and joining in a hula dance whenever the dancers moved in their direction or pointed toward them. Those on the right were enjoying the excitement of the dance and show with their children. The experience at the luau proves that every individual has emotional energy and that the intensity differs from individual to individual. Emotional intelligence is the synergy that is generated by managing emotions. It is an individual human process for achieving desired performance outcomes and differs from person to person. The three groups at the luau exhibited different emotional intensity and synergy levels to achieve their desired performance outcomes. The synergy of emotional intelligence helps individuals to achieve desired performance outcomes. The three groups at the luau had three different desired outcomes. The group near the bar used high-intensity energy, the group on the left side of the stage used moderate-intensity energy, and the group on the right used low-intensity energy. Understanding how one uses emotional intelligence consciously or unconsciously depends upon the emotional intensity and triggering events. Technologies such as AI are critical in influencing the intensity at which we use energy. An increase or decrease in intensity depends on the situation and individual abilities and capabilities.

Total Intelligence and AI

As discussed earlier in this chapter, total intelligence equals IQ, EQ, and UQ. However, Artificial Intelligence (AI) has become part of our total intelligence because of significant advancements in computing technology. The following exhibit shows the variable involved in total intelligence.

Exhibit-15: Total Intelligence

$$TIQ = IQ + EQ + AI + UQ$$

©2016 Mohammed R. Ahmed

Let's assume you are traveling from point A to B and reviewed your maps to prepare for the trip. The problem is you may not remember all the street names and turns to reach the destination. However, the vehicle you rented for the trip has an AI-supported navigation system. You can reach the destination on time without stress using the AI-supported system. Lower stress lowers the intensity of energy use.

AI technology is incorporated into phones, watches, automobiles, home appliances, and more to provide convenience and assistance. We have daily mental, physical, and emotional tasks, and we can incorporate AI in all our lives. There is a growing fear about the power and misuse of technology, which is a valid concern, and we need to set rules to make sure it is not causing harm to anyone. If AI technology is used ethically where needed in personal and professional life, it will lead to the road to success.

Artificial intelligence (AI) is a system designed by humans to perform mental, physical, and emotional tasks. It can solve problems using logic, apply knowledge to enhance capabilities and learn and apply knowledge to produce desired outcomes, among other mind abilities. Technology will never control us because we can turn off the technology by pressing the off button. AI systems are designed to solve problems and accomplish tasks, and they have learning capabilities and are additional tools for achieving success. Success is achieving your goals and requires a strategy for managing your energy and accomplishing specific goals. We will review the success in the next chapter.

SUCCESS

Happiness is the mental and emotional state that results in the sensation of succeeding and living a good life. It is a feeling of success, joy, accomplishment, and satisfaction.

Success is accomplishing your goals by managing energy and performing goal-specific tasks successfully. We focus on energy management because it builds the foundation for achieving positive outcomes in whatever areas the success is explored. For example, if we build a good foundation, we can use the foundation to build a two-bedroom, three, or two-story house. The same argument can be made that when individuals learn to manage energy for positive outcomes, they can use the learned approach to succeed in any field they enter or tasks they take to accomplish.

Have you ever wondered about a smart and friendly classmate from the school who you recently discovered that he/she is struggling to survive and losing his/her job? In this digital and knowledge-based economy, businesses seek people who can use their energy and add synergy to their business. The competition is fierce in the job market, and the marketplace is like a war zone. Individuals fail because they lack understanding of how to use their energy for positive outcomes and how to manage individual energy.

In a free society, we can choose what we want to accomplish and have the energy to do so. A rational person sets goals to achieve positive outcomes from using energy. To achieve these goals, we need to understand the areas that consume high energy, resulting in positive or negative outcomes to succeed. The areas include personal growth, emotions, trust, responsibility, learning, dreams, and intelligence. We also need a strategy for achieving specific goals. A strategy is a plan for accomplishing goals. Strategies can be offensive or defensive. We need offensive and defensive strategies to maximize the positive outcomes and minimize the negative outcomes from using energy. We can learn energy management from sports teams and offensive and defensive strategies. This is because sports teams focus on using energy management in physical, mental, and emotional tasks. Sports teams cannot win the championship by only using energy in physical tasks.

The sports teams compete to win championships, just as individuals compete to succeed in life. We can learn about the strategies from football, soccer, baseball, cricket, and other sports. In the Super Bowl or World Cup, the two teams compete to win the championship, a positive outcome for one team. The team's goal is to beat their opponent and win the championship. It is no different from an individual competing for jobs and wanting to beat their opponents in the job market. Like individuals, sports teams have a purpose, goals, and strategies to achieve these goals. Two Strategies that millions will witness on the field at the Super Bowl or the World Cup are the defensive and offensive strategies of the competing teams.

As you know, to win the championship, a team must be successful in both its defensive and offensive strategies. For example, a team's offensive strategy may lead to a touchdown or a goal, putting the score on the board. Also, the other team scores if the team's defense strategy is unsuccessful. On the other hand, if its defense strategy successfully prevents the other team from scoring, and its offensive strategy results in no score, the team still will not achieve its goal of winning the game. A defensive strategy in sports is to hold the other team from scoring, and an offensive strategy is to score against the other team. In our personal lives, we learn from football, soccer, and other sports that we need to focus on defensive and offensive strategies to maximize positive outcomes. We need to focus on the energy used by internal triggers to result in positive outcomes, and the energy used by external triggers also results in positive outcomes so that the benefits from using energy are maximized.

Let's revisit my encounter with the panhandler outside the hotel near the convention center. My goal was to give a successful presentation at the meeting. My strategy was to review and rehearse the presentation and arrive at the meeting before the scheduled time. While walking, I encountered an external trigger from the panhandler and used my energy for an offensive or defensive strategy to help me accomplish the goal. The external trigger did not change my goal; the goal was to give a good presentation and be there before the scheduled time. When panhandler showed anger at me, one of my offensive strategies was to respond with anger. I knew I would have wasted my energy, and the outcome would be negative. My offensive strategy was politely responding to him and saying I had no cash. The defensive strategy was to keep walking so he would calm down and find somebody else. All the other offensive and defensive strategies would have exhausted my energy, and I may be late for the meeting. It may have impacted my presentation because of the continued interaction with the panhandler, walking back, and reporting to the hotel concierge about the encounter. Interpreting internal and external triggers, allocating energy, and implementing the right defensive and offensive strategies resulted in a positive outcome, which was a successful presentation. The panhandler was unsuccessful in achieving his goals. He did not manage his energy, resulting in a negative outcome because he was probably reported by someone and was banned from the area because he was not near the hotel or convention center for the next two days.

Your goal should be to use minimum energy and generate maximum positive outcomes. To stay on the road to success, you must continually determine whether your energy management strategy results in positive outcomes. If your strategy is not successful, learn why and reengineer it. Your strategy should minimize energy consumption for negative outcomes and use energy to maximize positive outcomes. Lastly, managing your emotions changes your energy use and will take you on the road to success.

ABOUT THE AUTHOR

Mohammed R Ahmed

Dr. Mohammed R Ahmed has taught undergraduate, master's, and doctoral programs at various universities and colleges for over 35 years. He has served as a dissertation chair and committee member for several doctoral students pursuing doctoral degrees. His experience includes teaching graduate corporate clusters at several Fortune 500 companies and international corporate clusters, KSC, and military facilities.

His research is focused on individual self-improvement and business management. He has developed a basic emotional intelligence model, the 5Ps of Management, a simplified business model, and the Micro-cell economic model. He has also developed a new leadership theory named Emerging Leadership Theory (ELT), which he presented at the 2012 Academy of Management Conferences and received recognition.

He has been a member of the Professional Management Association for more than 30 years and attends meetings regularly. He has presented papers and served as a reviewer for the annual conferences and peer-reviewed journals in business and management. He was also a keynote speaker at the annual meetings. For the last thirty-five years, he has presented papers and offered workshops at international business and management conferences in Asia, Europe, the Middle East, and North America.

www.ingramcontent.com/pod-product-compliance
Lightning Source LLC
LaVergne TN
LVHW010611070526
838199LV00063BA/5139